Samsung Galaxy S24 Ultra User Guide

The Comprehensive Step-by-Step Instruction and Illustrated Manual for Beginners & Seniors to Master the Samsung Galaxy S24 Ultra with Tips and Tricks

Shawn Blaine

Table of Contents

Introduction

The Samsung Galaxy S24 Ultra is the top-of-the-line smartphone in the S24 Series, and the only smartphone in the lineup that supports the S Pen stylus. The device is packed with lots of amazing AI-powered capabilities, stunning camera features, and other amazing components to improve the user's experience.

It has a 6.8-inch OLED panel. Compared to its predecessor, the screen is less curved and the bezel is now thinner.

The main camera stands at 200 megapixels, while the ultrawide camera is loaded with 12 mega-pixels with a 3x telephoto camera that stands at 10MP.

For photography lovers, Samsung has upgraded its low-light shooting which is often tagged "Nightography," and most applications on the smartphone now support Super HDR and AI capabilities which include background removal and image remastering.

One of the most notable AI improvements to the Galaxy S24 Ultra's photography is its generative editing capabilities. This feature allows you to reposition objects in an image or even extend the image's edges.

You can even slow down and flatten your video clips by just long-pressing the video thanks to the instant slo-mo feature that is powered by AI.

The smartphone runs on Android 14, although it is laced with Samsung's One UI 6.1. Also, Samsung has included Qualcomm's Snapdragon 8 Gen 3 as the chipset for the devices in the Galaxy S24 series. It has a 12GB RAM.

Samsung has retained 5,000 mAh for the battery. However, it has improved longevity than its predecessor. For wired charging, you get 45W, while wireless charging offers 15W abilities.

The eye-catching features of the Galaxy S24 Ultra are the AI capabilities. When having a conversation through phone calls or messaging apps, you can get a real-time translation of what the other person is saying thanks to Call Assist and Chat translation.

Thanks to Browser Assist, you can quickly get a summary of a large chunk of text on a webpage when surfing the internet via the Samsung Internet application with just a click of a few menus.

Interestingly, the AI feature can also check for grammar and errors in your sentence compositions and recommend ways to improve your writing.

Also, AI can help you reformat your texts on the Samsung Notes app and even straighten your texts that are written with the S Pen.

Thanks to the Circle to Search features, users can find out more about an object by simply long-pressing the Home button and drawing a circle on the screen, and then Google will pull up the result.

There are so many AI-powered features to help you maximize your Samsung Galaxy S24 Ultra and become a better smartphone user even if you've never used a Samsung or Android smartphone before. This user guide is loaded with lots of camera and photograph tips and tricks, including basic, advanced, and AI tips to help you master your smartphone like a pro.

Chapter One

Setup Samsung Galaxy Ultra

After purchasing and unboxing your Galaxy s24 Ultra, you'll have to charge it and slot your SIM card into the SIM card tray. After that, you can then power on the device and commence the setup.

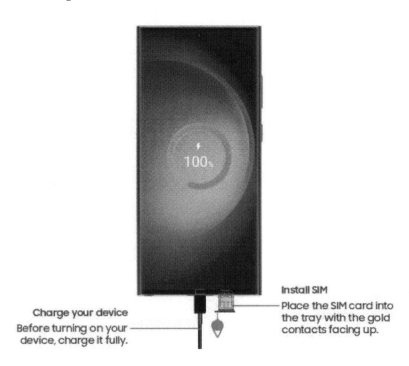

Install SIM
Place the SIM card into the tray with the gold contacts facing up.

Charge your device
Before turning on your device, charge it fully.

- Start by long-tapping the Power button until the device screen displays the

Samsung Galaxy image, then remove your hands.

- Choose a language.
- Afterward, hit the "**Start**" button.

- Review the next page, then select "**Next**."

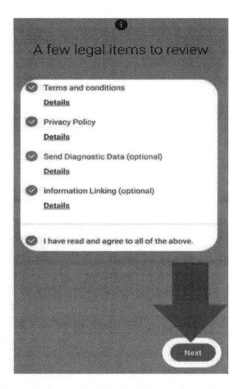

- Hit **"Next"** on the **"Phone Activation"** menu. Go ahead and insert the account PIN if needed.

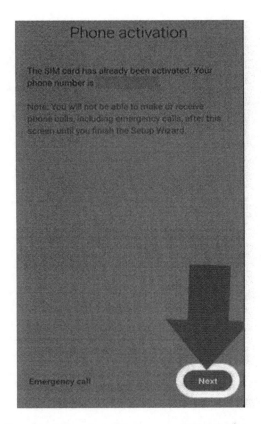

- Proceed by choosing your Wi-Fi network and inserting the password from the **"Set up Wi-Fi"** menu. Hit **"Skip"** to configure it later.

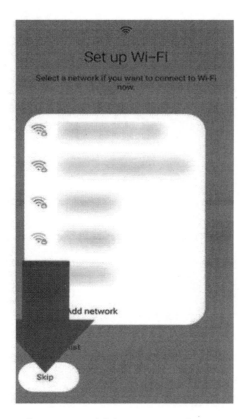

- On the menu asking you to "**Copy apps & data**," hit on "**Next**" or "**Don't copy**."
- Go ahead and sign into your Google account. However, if you don't have one, go ahead and create one. To do this later, hit "**Skip**." If you have your Google account credentials, hit "**Next**" or press "**Create account**."

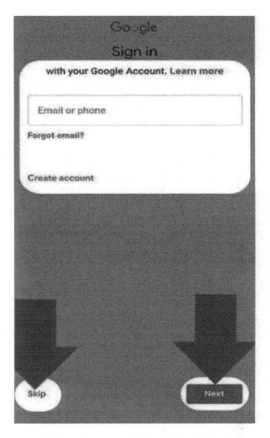

- Proceed by turning on or off your desired features on the "**Google Services**" page.
- Afterward, hit "**Accept**."

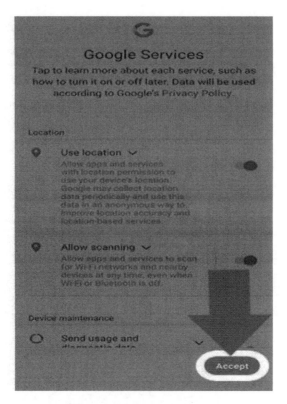

- The "**Protect your phone**" menu will display and you'll be required to choose an option to secure your device. To perform this action, later on, hit "**Not now**.

- Proceed by enabling or disabling the location or application information. Afterward, hit "**Accept**."

- Up next, hit "**Agree**" or "**Skip**."

- Follow up by tapping "**Accept**" or "**Skip**" on the "**Digital Secure**" menu.

- On the "**Samsung account**" menu, go ahead and insert your details to sign in or create an account. Hit **"Skip"** to do it later.

- Once the completion menu appears, hit **"Done."**

Enable Wireless Power Sharing

With wireless power sharing, you'll be able to wirelessly charge your supported Samsung devices using your Galaxy Ultra smartphone. While using wireless power sharing, certain features will be disabled on your smartphone. Ensure your Galaxy Ultra has a thirty percent charge before trying to use wireless power sharing. The features work with most Qi-certified devices that support the power share feature.

- Launch the Settings app.
- After that, hit "**Battery and device care**."
- Next up, choose "**Battery**."
- From there, press "**Wireless power sharing**."
- Hit on "**Battery limit**."
- Then select a percentage. Immediately the gadget you're charging gets to this charge percentage, the wireless power sharing feature will automatically disable.
- Tap to enable it.
- To start the wireless power sharing, ensure that your Galaxy Ultra is facing down, then position the supported device on the back of your Galaxy Ultra smartphone to charge. Once the

charging starts, you should see an alert
or it'll vibrate.

Turn on your device

When attempting to power on your Galaxy
smartphone, simply press the Side key.

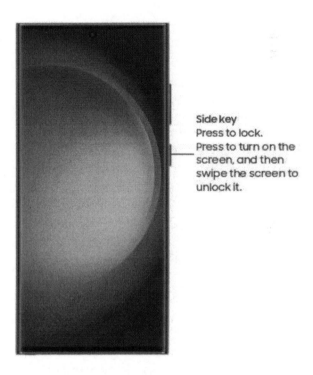

Side key
Press to lock.
Press to turn on the
screen, and then
swipe the screen to
unlock it.

- Long-tap the Side key to power on your
  Galaxy Ultra.

Power off device

- To power it off, long-tap the Side and Volume down keys simultaneously.
- Then press "⏻ **Power off**."
- Next up, hit "**Confirm**."

Restart the device

- To restart the smartphone, long-tap the Side and Volume down keys simultaneously.
- Then, hit "⟳ **Restart**."
- Next up, press "**Confirm**."

Bring data from an old device

If you intend to move movies, calendars, contacts, images, audio, etc., you're your older device ensure you download the Smart Switch app. With the app, you can transfer your files using a PC, USB cable, or Wi-Fi.

- Launch the Settings app.
- Then hit on "**Accounts and backup**."

- From there, touch "**Bring data from old device**."
- Go through the onscreen guide and choose the files to transfer.

Side Key Settings

If needed, you can change the shortcuts that appear when you press the Side key.

Double press

This lets you adjust the feature that opens up whenever you press the Side key twice.

- Launch the Settings app.
- Afterward, press "**Advanced features**."
- Up next, touch "**Side key**."
- From there, hit "**Double press**" to turn on this feature.
- Then, choose "**Open app**" or "**Quick launch camera**."

Press and hold

This lets you adjust the feature that opens whenever you long-tap the Side key.

- Launch the Settings app.

- Afterward, press "**Advanced features**."
- Up next, touch "**Side key**."
- Underneath the "**Press and hold**" submenu, hit on "**Power off menu**" or "**Wake Bixby**."

Chapter Two

Set up Accounts

Adding a Samsung, Google, or other email provider account gives you access to backup and link your contacts, and calendars, including other features.

Add a Google Account
- Launch the Settings app.
- From there, press "**Accounts and backup**."
- Then choose "**Manage accounts**."
- Up next, press "**Add account**."
- Now, hit "**Google**."

Add a Samsung account
- Launch the Settings app.
- From there, press "**Samsung account**."

Add an Outlook account
- Launch the Settings app.
- From here, press "**Accounts and backup**."
- Afterward, press "**Manage accounts**."
- Up next, press "**Add account**."

- Here, select "**Outlook**."

Samsung Pass

Samsung Pass stores your biometric information and then lets you access your desired services without having to sign up.

- Launch the Settings app.
- Now, hit "**Security and privacy**."
- After that, press "**Samsung Pass**."
- Proceed by logging into your Samsung account, then register your biometric information.

Secure Folder

Secure folders let you encrypt files, applications, and content that are too confidential for public view.

- Launch the Settings app.
- Then press "**Security and privacy**."
- Afterward, hit "**Secure Folder**."
- Go through the prompts to finalize the setup.

Private Share

Private Share lets you share files securely and then disable the sharing of them with other people.

- Go to Settings.
- From there, hit "**Security and privacy**."
- Afterward, choose "**Secure Folder**."
- Next up, hit "**Private share**."
- Go through the guide to add files.

Samsung Blockchain Keystore

Samsung Blockchain Keystore lets users manage their blockchain private key.

- Navigate to Settings.
- Then, press "**Security and privacy**."
- Next up, hit "**Samsung Blockchain Keystore**."
- Go through the guide to import your keys. Alternately, you can set up another cryptocurrency wallet.

Set up the Samsung Wallet app

Samsung Wallet can be used to store your credit card information, transit keys, IDs, and many more. It's your digital wallet. And you can access Samsung Pay from there as well.

- Head to the Samsung Wallet app.
- Go through the information, then hit "**Continue**" to commence the setup. Authorize any required permission.
- Proceed by inserting your Samsung account details.
- Afterward, choose "**Continue**."
- You'll be required to add your fingerprints if you've not done that already. Hit "**Register fingerprints**." Go through the prompts to register your fingerprint. Alternately, you can select to use a **PIN**.
- Proceed by positioning your finger on the fingerprint sensor to authenticate your identity after you've registered your fingerprints.
- Next up, hit "**All the time**" if you prefer using the Wallet for contactless payments or "**Don't use**" if you intend not to use it.
- Afterward, choose "**Done**."

- You should see a new pop-up, hit **"Replace"** if you desire your default payment to be the Samsung Pay application rather than Google Pay.

Backup and restore

Having your data backed up will save you from permanently losing your files if your smartphone develops a fault or crashes beyond repair.

Samsung account

You can backup your files to the Samsung Cloud.

- Head to the Settings app.
- Then, press **"Accounts and backup."**
- Hit on **"Back up data"** underneath the Samsung Cloud menu.
- Hit on **"Restore data"** to retrieve your backup data.

Google Account

The process is the same if you prefer to backup with your Google account.

- Head to the Settings app.

- Then, press "**Accounts and backup**."
- Hit on "**Back up data**" underneath the Google Drive menu.

External storage transfer

You can also back up your files with an external storage device by connecting your Galaxy Ultra to a USB cable.

- Head to the Settings app.
- Then, press "**Accounts and backup**."
- Lastly, hit "**External storage transfer**."

Chapter Three

How to Navigate your device

When navigating your Galaxy Ultra, ensure you tap the touch screen gently, as excessive force can damage the screen. You can zoom in and out, swipe, tap, drag, and drop, among other gesture actions.

Tap

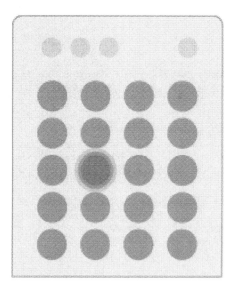

- Gently press icons to choose or open them.
- Tap the icon to choose it.
- Tap twice on a photo to zoom in/out.

Swipe

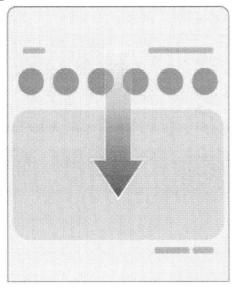

- Gently move your finger across your Galaxy Ultra screen.
- Swipe the display to unlock your Galaxy phone.
- Swipe the smartphone screen to scroll across the Home screens or menu.

Drag and drop

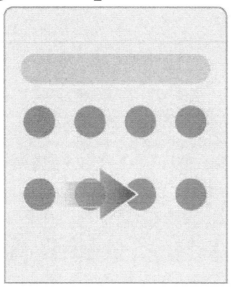

- Long-tap an icon, then drag it to a new spot on the screen.
- Drag an application shortcut to move it to your Home screen.
- To change a widget position, simply drag and drop it into the new location.

Zoom in and out

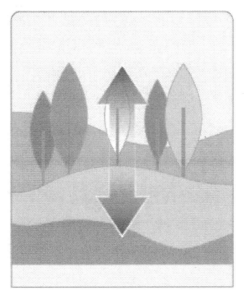

- Drag your thumb and forefinger close or spread them apart on your Galaxy Ultra screen to zoom in and out.
- To zoom in, go ahead and drag your thumb and forefinger away from each other on the display.
- To zoom out, drag your thumb and forefinger together on your phone display.

Touch and hold

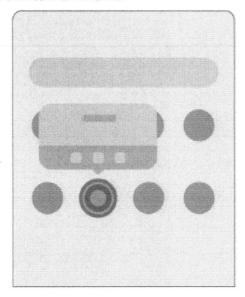

Touch and hold are also known as press and hold, long-tap, or long-press.

- Long-tap an icon to activate them.
- Long-press an input field to show options.
- Press and hold a Home screen to edit it.

Navigation Bar

To navigate your Galaxy Ultra smartphone, you can use the navigation buttons at the button of the display or the full-screen gestures.

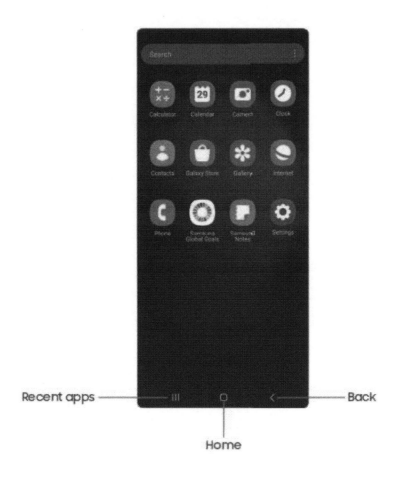

Recent apps ——— ||| ○ ‹——— Back

Home

Enable Navigation Buttons

The Recent apps, Home, and Back buttons in the photo above are the navigation buttons. You can use them for easy and quick navigation.

- Launch the Settings app.
- Then hit "**Display**."
- Afterward, choose "**Navigation bar**."
- Then press "**Buttons**."

- Proceed by pressing an option below
  "Button order" to pick the position on
  the display where the Recent apps and
  Back buttons will appear.

Enable Navigation Gestures

To avoid interruptions from the navigation
buttons while using your smartphone, hide
them and utilize swipe (navigation gestures)
instead.

- Launch the Settings app.
- Then hit **"Display."**
- Afterward, choose **"Navigation bar."**
- From there, hit **"Swipe gestures"** to
  activate it.

To customize the swipe gesture, choose an
option:

- **Gesture hint**: Show lines at the lower
  part of the display where you can find
  each screen gesture.
- **Block gestures with S Pen**: This
  option disables the navigation gestures
  when using the S Pen.
- **Show button to hide keyboard**:
  Selecting this option will make your
  smartphone show an icon on the lower
  right edge of the display to mask the
  keyboard when your Galaxy Ultra is in
  portrait mode.

- **More options**: This enables you to pick a gesture type and sensitivity.

Chapter Four

Customize your Home Screen

You can personalize your phone's home screen by adding your favorite applications, changing the screen layout, removing items you dislike, and so on.

Add App Icons

When you press an app icon, it'll launch that application.

- From the Apps menu, long-press an app icon.

- Then choose "⌂ **Add to Home.**"

Removing an icon

- Long-tap an app icon from the Home screen.

- Up next, hit "🗑 **Remove.**"
- This action only takes off the application from the Home screen, it doesn't delete the application from your smartphone.

Add Wallpaper

You can personalize the appearance of your Galaxy Ultra by changing the image that is displayed on your Home and Lock screens.

- Long-tap a blank area on your Home screen.

- From there, hit " 🖼️ **Wallpaper and style**."

- Press the Home screen photos to customize them or go ahead and touch any of the options below to pick a wallpaper:

- **Change wallpapers**: Select a wallpaper from the various options. Alternately, you can download it from the Galaxy Themes.

- **Color palette**: Touch a palette depending on the colors of the wallpaper you choose.

Add Themes

You can also apply a theme to both your Home and Lock screens.

- Long-tap a blank area on your Home screen.

- Then choose " 🖌️ **Themes**."

- Go ahead and choose a theme to check it out and install it.

View Themes

- To view your downloaded themes, hit on  "**Menu**."
- Then choose "**My stuff**."
- Now choose "**Themes**" to view your downloaded themes.
- From there, choose a theme.
- Afterward, select "**Apply**" to use the theme on your smartphone.

Add Icons

If desired, you can change the default icon appearance of your smartphone by replacing it with your preferred one.

- Long-tap a blank area on your Home screen.
- Then choose "**Themes**."
- Now, choose "**Icons**."
- Proceed by pressing an icon to check it out and install it.

View Downloaded Icons

- To see your downloaded icons, press " **Menu**."

- Then select "My stuff."
- After this, choose "Icons."
- To apply the icon, select it, and press "**Apply**."

Add Widgets

Widgets provide swift access to information or applications.

- Long-press an empty section on your Home screen.
- Then choose "⬜◯ **Widgets**."
- Go ahead and press on a widget to open it.
- Proceed by swiping to the widget you intend to apply to your Home screen, then choose "**Add**."

Customize Widgets

After adding a widget, you'll be able to change its location on the screen and its function.

- Long-press on a widget on your Home screen, then choose an option:
- **Settings**: To personalize the function or layout of the widget.
- **Create stack**: Place additional widgets that are of equal size to stack them in the same location.

- **App info**: To access the widget permission, usage, etc.
- **Remove**: To get rid of the widget from your phone display.

Adjust Home Screen Settings

You can personalize your Home and Apps screens further by adjusting the layout, adding new apps to it, and lots more.

- Long-tap anywhere on your Home screen.
- Then choose "**Settings**."
- Select any of the options below:
- **Folder grid**: To adjust the order in which folders appear on the screen.
- **Home screen layout**: To configure your Galaxy Ultra to have dedicated Home and Apps screens, or make all your apps appear on the Home screen.
- **Lock Home screen layout**: To set the icons on your Home screen from being deleted or moved.
- **Home screen grid**: Select how icons appear on your Home screen.
- **Apps screen grid**: Select how icons appear on your Apps screen.

- **App icon badges**: Turn on to display badges on applications with active alerts/notifications.

Enable Easy Mode

When you switch to Easy mode on your Galaxy Ultra, your text and icons will appear bigger. It is ideal for seniors.

- Launch the Settings app.
- Then hit "**Display.**"
- From there, choose "**Easy mode.**"

- Afterward, press to activate it.
- Some options will display:
- **High contrast keyboard**: Allows you to pick a keyboard with a standout contrast color.
- **Touch and hold delay**: Choose the duration it'll take for a continuous touch to be detected as a long-tap.

Manage the Status Bar

The Status bar offers a quick way to view some features. It also offers device info and alerts for notifications.

Status icons

Battery full	Charging	Mute	Vibrate

Airplane mode	Bluetooth active	Location active	Alarm

Notification icons

Missed calls	Call in progress	New message	Voicemail

New email	Download	Upload	App update

You can customize the Status bar

- Launch the Settings app.
- Then choose "**Notifications**."
- From there, choose "**Advanced Settings**."
- Then select an option to edit under the "**Status bar**" section.

Notification Panel

Just like the Status bar, the notification panel provides a faster way to access and enable some settings.

Quick settings

Device settings

Notification cards

See the Notification Panel

Regardless of the screen you're viewing, you can open the Notification panel right away.

- To show the Notification panel, just swipe down on your Galaxy Ultra screen.
- Press an icon to open it.
- If you need to clear a notification, drag it left/right.
- To clear the entire notifications, press **"Clear."**
- Hit on "Notification settings" to personalize notifications.

- To exit the Notification panel, simply drag up from the bottom of your display.

  Alternately, press "< **Back**."

Quick Settings

The Notification Panel offers a faster way to open the settings menu of certain features, which is why it is also called Quick Settings.

When you access the notification panel, you'll see some icons; these icons are shortcuts to their settings.

| Wi-Fi | Sound | Bluetooth | Auto rotate |
| Airplane mode | Location | Power saving | Dark mode |

- To show the Notification panel, simply drag down on the Status bar.
- Proceed by swiping down once more from the screen top to show the Quick settings.
- Then press a quick setting icon to enable or disable it.
- Long-tap a quick setting icon to move to its settings menu.

Enable Always On Display

With Always On Display, which is abbreviated as "AOD," users can view time and date and see missed calls and notifications without having to unlock their Galaxy Ultra.

- Launch the Settings app.
- Then choose "**Lock screen**."
- Afterward, hit "**Always On Display**."

- Go ahead and press ⬤◯ to activate the feature.
- Proceed by selecting **Clock style**, **Auto brightness**, **Screen orientation**, etc., to customize Always On Display.

Always On Display Themes
You can also include custom themes for AOD.

- Long-tap anywhere on your Home screen.
- Then choose "**Themes**."
- Hit on "AODs." You can hit on an AOD to check it out and even install it.
- To access downloaded themes, choose " ☰ **Menu**," then choose "**My stuff**," and select "**AODs**."
- To apply an AOD, select it, then choose "**Apply**."

Change the device language

- Head to the Settings app.
- Afterward, hit "**General management**."
- From there, choose "**Language**."
- Tap the plus button, then choose a language from the menu.
- Go ahead and hit "**Set as default**."
- If you intend to switch to a different language from the menu, click on it, then hit "**Apply**."

Chapter Five

How to use S Pen

With the S Pen, you can sketch, compose notes and open applications. However, ensure not to place it close to a magnet.

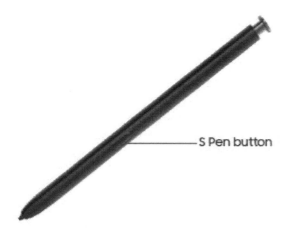

S Pen button

Remove the S Pen

For convenience and ease of access, Samsung has stored the S Pen at the bottom of your Galaxy Ultra.

Also, it charges the S Pen when it's slotted at the bottom. You can use gestures with the S Pen to perform some functions.

To take out the S Pen, press it inward, then pull it out.

Air View

To get a sneak peek at the contents or see some details relating to something on the display, simply hover your S Pen across the screen. You can access the following functionalities through Air View:

- Get a sneak peek at a video and jump to a particular scene when you look across the timeline.
- Get a peek at an email before you open it.
- View the photos in an album or zoom in on an image.
- See a button's or icon's name.
- See the description of a button or icon.

Air Actions

You can use the S Pen to carry out remote tasks by pressing the button or through movement or gestures. Also, you may even use it to add shortcuts to some applications, perform some tasks, move across your phone screen, etc.

To use Air actions, ensure that the S Pen is connected.

- Launch the Settings app.
- From there, press "**Advanced features**."
- Then hit "**S Pen**."
- Up next, hit "**Air actions**" to activate it.

Hold the S Pen button shortcut

By default, pressing and holding the S Pen will open the Camera application, but you can change that.

- Launch the Settings app.
- From there, press "**Advanced features**."
- After this, press "**S Pen**."
- Now, choose "**Air actions**"
- Afterward, hit the "**Press and hold Pen button**."

- Then press to activate it.

Anywhere Actions

You can customize your S Pen to perform a task or open a menu when you make gestures such as a shake, up and down movement, or move the S Pen left or right.

- Launch the Settings app.
- Then hit "**Advanced features**."
- From there, hit "**S Pen**."
- Afterward, hit "**Air actions**."
- Then press the Gesture icon underneath the "**Anywhere actions**" option to personalize the shortcut.

App Actions

You'll be able to set your S Pen to perform certain actions in some applications.

- Launch the Settings app.
- Then hit "**Advanced features**."
- From there, press "**S Pen**."
- Now, touch "**Air actions**."
- Proceed by pressing an application to access its available shortcuts.

- Then press to activate the shortcuts when using the application.

General App Actions

The General App Actions menu allows you to edit some actions when you're using the camera and other media applications that are not stated in the application action list.

- Launch the Settings app.
- Afterward, press "**Advanced features**."
- From there, choose "**S Pen**."
- Now, touch "**Air actions**."
- Underneath the "**General app actions**," choose an action to modify it.

Screen Off Memo

With the screen off memo, you don't need to turn on your Galaxy Ultra screen before you can write on it.

- Launch the Settings app.
- Then hit "**Advanced features**."
- Go ahead and choose "**S Pen**."
- Afterward, choose "**Screen off memos**" and enable it.
- Take out the S Pen when your smartphone screen is off, then start writing on the display.
- Go ahead and choose an option such as Eraser, Color, or Pen settings to personalize your memo.
- Afterward, hit "**Save**."

Pin to Always On Display

- While on the screen off memo, hit on "**Pin to Always on Display**."
- From there, hit "**Pin to Always On Display**."

Air Command

You can open some menus quickly by using some S-Pen gestures.

- Press the " **Air command**" or position your S Pen close to the screen to make the pointer pop up.
- Afterward, tap the S Pen button.
- Proceed by selecting an option such as Smart select, AR Doodle, Create note, PENUP, Add, Settings, and more.

Create Note

You can navigate to the Samsung Notes app directly from the Air command menu.

- Press "Air command."
- Then hit "**Create note**."

Smart Select

Regardless of the screen, you're currently viewing, you can copy its contents and store them on your Gallery application or share them with other people.

- Press "Air command."
- Then hit "**Smart select**."
- Proceed by clicking on a shape.
- Go ahead and drag your S Pen to choose its content. Some options such as Draw, Share, Auto select, etc., will pop up.
- Choose an option, then press "**Save**."

AR Doodle

With Air command, users can sketch doodles using augmented reality.

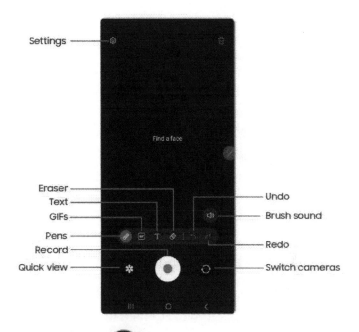

- Press " **Air command.**"

- Then hit " **AR Doodle.**"

- Proceed by choosing the front/rear cameras by hitting " **Switch cameras.**"

- Go ahead and place the camera such that your target appears in the middle of the display.

- Then use the S Pen to sketch the doodle.

- Afterward, hit "**Record.**"

PENUP

With the S Pen, users can draw, edit, and color their drawings, as well as share them with friends.

- Press "Air command."
- Then hit "**PENUP**."

How to use Bixby

Bixby was created by Samsung as a personal assistant. Bixby is powered by artificial learning and can learn your day-to-day activities, set up alarms and reminders, read online news, and even solve mathematical tasks. It works just like Alexa and Google Assistant. To open Bixby, press the Apps list button on your home screen or long-tap the Side key.

Bixby Vision

Samsung has integrated Bixby into the camera and Internet application to enhance users' photographic and browsing experiences. It can be used to translate, shop, and even detect landmarks and detours.

Camera

Bixby Vision provides users with a clear understanding of any object they capture through the Camera app.

- Launch the Camera app .
- Then select "**More**."
- Afterward, hit "**Bixby Vision**."
- Proceed by following the prompts.

Gallery

You can use Bixby Vision to know more about images that are stored in your Gallery app.

- Launch the Gallery app .
- Click on an image to view it.
- Then hit " **Bixby Vision**."
- Go through the prompts.

Internet

With Bixby Vision, you can discover more about any photo that you see while browsing with the Internet app.

- Launch the Internet app and navigate to an image.

- Long-tap the image to bring up the pop-up menu.
- Next, press "**Search with Bixby Vision**."
- Go through the prompt to finish.

Chapter Six

Manage Biometric Security

Adding biometric security to your smartphone ensures that only your fingerprints, face ID, or PIN can be used to unlock your smartphone, ensuring that nobody gains unauthorized access to your accounts.

Set up a basic phone lock screen

You can protect your smartphone by adding a basic phone lock such as a PIN, pattern, or password.

- Launch the Settings app.
- Then hit "**Lock screen**."
- From there, choose "**Screen lock type**." The screen lock types to choose from include **Password**, **Pattern**, **Swipe**, **PIN**, and **None**.

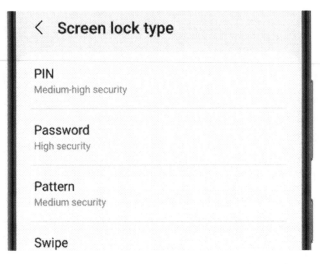

- Proceed by choosing your preferred screen lock, then go through the prompts to finish.

Set up and use fingerprint unlock

You can enhance the security of your Galaxy Ultra by registering your fingerprint, which ensures that only your fingerprints can unlock your smartphone.

- Launch the Settings app.
- Then hit "**Security and privacy**."
- From there, choose "**Biometrics**."
- Afterward, choose "**Fingerprints**."

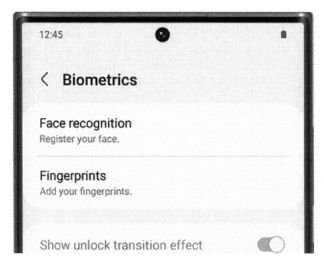

- Proceed by entering your lock screen (Password, Pattern, Swipe, PIN) information. If you're yet to add a basic lock screen, you may be asked to create one. Review the information, then choose "**Continue**."
- Go ahead and follow the prompts to add your fingerprint. Ensure to completely cover the fingerprint sensor when adding your fingerprint.
- Afterward, press "**Done**."
- Ensure you toggle on the switch next to "**Fingerprint unlock**" to activate the feature.
- Whenever you wish to unlock your smartphone with your finger, press the display or tap the Power or Side key. Go ahead and position the registered finger on your phone's fingerprint scanner.

Once the device detects your fingerprint, it'll automatically unlock.

- To rename the registered fingerprint, hit **"Rename a fingerprint**," then choose the fingerprint, insert a new name, and choose "**Save**."

Add additional fingerprints

Users can register multiple fingerprints that can be used to unlock their Galaxy Ultra.

- Launch the Settings app.
- Then hit "**Security and privacy**."
- From there, choose "**Biometrics**."
- Afterward, choose "**Fingerprints**."
- Proceed by entering your screen lock information.
- Afterward, hit "**Add fingerprint**."

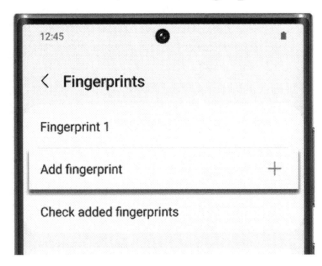

- Go through the prompts, then hit "**Done**."

Remove a fingerprint from your device

Removing a fingerprint from your Galaxy Ultra is simple.

- Launch the Settings app.
- Then hit "**Security and privacy**."
- From there, choose "**Biometrics**."
- Afterward, choose "**Fingerprints**."
- Proceed by entering your security information, then choose the fingerprint you intend to remove.
- Next up, choose "**Remove**."

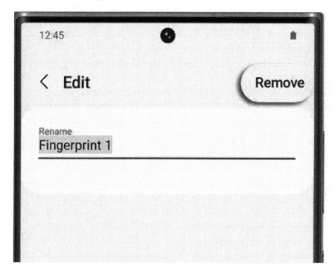

- Hit on "**Remove**" once more to finish.

Set up Facial recognition

Some people prefer to use their faces to unlock their smartphones. If you like that option, then you can register your face on your smartphone. However, ensure you've already added a password, PIN, or pattern.

- Launch the Settings app.
- Afterward, press "**Security and privacy**."
- From there, choose "**Biometrics**."
- Up next, touch "**Face recognition**."
- Proceed by entering your PIN/password.
- Then choose "**Continue**."
- Position your Galaxy Ultra about ten to twenty inches away and place your face within the circle displayed on your screen. Keep holding until the progress bar clocks 100%.
- To remove the registered face from your smartphone, navigate to the "**Face recognition**" menu in the settings app, then choose "**Remove face data**."
- To ensure that your Galaxy Ultra is only unlocked when your eyes are open, select "**Require open eyes**" and activate it.

Chapter Seven

How to use the Camera

The Camera application enables you to capture amazing photos and record stunning videos.

- To launch the Camera application, open the App list, then choose Camera.
- Alternatively, double-tap the Side key to launch the Camera app.

Navigate the camera screen

You can capture spectacular moments with your Galaxy Ultra front and back cameras.

- Launch the Camera app.
- Then press the screen where you prefer your camera to focus. Tapping on the screen will bring up a brightness scale. Go ahead and drag the slider to change the brightness.
- Swipe upward or downward on the screen to swiftly alternate between your phone's front and back cameras.
- To zoom accurately, press **1x** and choose an option from the bottom of the display.
- Swipe horizontally (left or right) to adjust the various shooting modes.
- Hit " **Settings**" to adjust the camera's settings.
- Afterward, press to capture.

Configure shooting mode

The Camera app offers different shooting modes for different effects and purposes; you can manually select or let the app use them for you.

Night portrait

You can still capture a high-resolution photo in the dark thanks to the Nightography features.

- Launch the Camera app.
- Proceed by swiping to and tapping "**MORE**."
- Afterward, choose "**NIGHT**."
- Go ahead and position your shot. To zoom in or out, pinch the display using your fingers. Otherwise, press 3x or 10x.
- Then hit "**Capture**."
- Alternatively, press the switch camera button to alternate to the front camera. Then hit "**Capture**" to snap a selfie.

Night video

You can also use the Nightography feature when recording videos on your phone.

- Launch the Camera app.
- Afterward, choose "**VIDEO**."
- Then press the crescent moon icon to turn on the Night shot.
- Next up, hit "**Record**" to start recording.
- A prompt will display telling you to keep your smartphone steady when recording.
- To discontinue the filming, press "**Stop**."

High-resolution photos

Images captured by your smartphone can reach as much as 200MB. When you share these images through social media applications, they could appear as files. However, you can fix this by adjusting the file size.

- Launch the Gallery app.
- Then choose your image.
- Afterward, press the pencil icon.
- Then choose the three vertical dots.
- Afterward, select "**Resize**."
- Proceed by choosing your preferred ratio.
- Now, choose "**Done**."
- Hit on the three vertical dots once more.
- Next up, press "**Save as copy**."

Expert RAW photos

The Expert RAW applications allow users to capture professional-level pictures.

- Launch the Camera app.
- Choose "**MORE**."
- From there, choose "**EXPERT RAW**."

- You'll be asked to download the app if you've not done so; click "**Install**."
- Authorize the required permissions if required. Then click on any of the picture options:
- **Astrophoto**: Click on the Astrophoto button (i.e., the constellation icon) at the upper right edge. Then click "**Show**" or "**Hide**" beside Sky guide, and turn on location accuracy if asked. Proceed by using the slider to configure the Duration. Afterward, position your camera and hit "**Capture**."
- **Multiple exposures**: Press the two-squares icon in the upper section of the display to utilize the various exposure options. Then hit "**Manual**" or "**Continuous**," which is besides "**Shutter**." Go ahead and select your preferred settings beside "**Overlay**."

Proceed by using the slider to adjust the exposures. Position your camera and hit **Capture**.

AR Zone

The Galaxy Ultra is loaded with some Augmented Reality features that can take your photo capture to a new level.

- Launch the Camera app.
- Proceed by swiping to "**MORE.**"
- Then choose "**AR Zone.**"

- Go ahead and choose any of the AR options: AR Emoji Stickers, AR Emoji Camera, Deco Pic, etc.

Space Zoom

Space Zoom allows users to capture crisp and clear images with as much as a hundred times magnification.

- Launch the Camera app.
- Then choose "**Zoom shortcut**." From here, you can choose a magnification setting.
- Proceed by positioning your target in the middle of the frame, then choose "

  Zoom lock" for quick and precise zoom focusing.

- Then hit ⬤ .

Record videos

Use your Galaxy Ultra to record natural and fluid videos.

- Launch the Camera app.
- Then swipe to "**Video**" mode.

- Next up, press the " ⬤ **Record**" button to start filming a video.

- Hit 🔲 to snap a photo while recording.

- To pause the recording, hit "

  Pause." To resume, hit "
  Resume."

- To discontinue recording, hit "
  Stop."

360 audio recording

You can get immersive 3D sound when you connect your Galaxy Ultra with supported Bluetooth headphones.

- Launch the Camera app.

- Then choose " Settings."
- From there, hit "**Advanced video options.**"
- Afterward, hit on "**360 audio recording**" to activate it.

Chapter Eight

How to use the Gallery

You can browse through all the images and videos stored on your Galaxy Ultra by navigating to the Gallery app.

Launch the Gallery app from the Apps list.

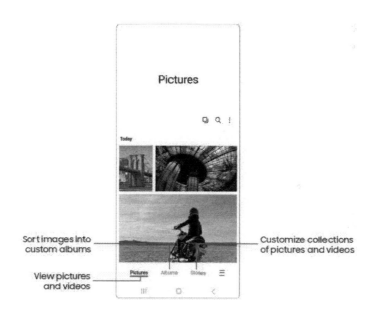

View pictures

The Gallery application is where you can locate the images that are stored on your Galaxy Ultra.

- Launch the Gallery app.

- Then choose "**Pictures**."
- Choose an image to view it. Proceed by swiping horizontally (left or right) to see other media content.

- Hit ⊙ **Bixby Vision** to utilize Bixby Vision on that particular image.

- Hit " ♡ **Add to Favorites**" to label the image as a favorite.

- Press " ⋮ " to view other options such as **Remaster picture**, **Print**, **Set as wallpaper**, **Details**, etc.

Edit pictures

You can improve your captured image by adding filters, adjusting tone, fine-tuning the color, and lots more using the built-in editing tools.

- Launch the Gallery app.
- Then choose "**Pictures**."
- Then select the image to see it.

- Afterward, hit the Edit ✎ button, then choose from the pop-up options: for the following options: **Filters**, **Decorations**, **Revert**, **Decorations**, etc.
- After editing, hit "**Save**."

Play video

Just like you do with images stored in the Gallery application, you can also you're your videos.

- Launch the Gallery app.
- Then choose "**Pictures**."
- Choose a video to view it. Go ahead and swipe horizontally (left or right) to see other media content.

- Press " ♡ **Add to Favorites**" to label the video as a favorite.

- Press " ⋮ " to view other options such as: **Set as wallpaper, Details, Set as Open in Video player**, etc.

- Hit ▶ to watch the video.

Video brightness

Adjusting the brightness of a video on your Galaxy Ultra is easy.

- Launch the Settings app.
- Then hit "**Advanced features**."
- From there, choose "**Video brightness**."
- Proceed by selecting an option.

Edit video

- Launch the Gallery app.
- Then choose **"Pictures."**
- Proceed by tapping a video to watch it.
- Then select ✐ **Edit**.
- Go ahead and choose your desired option: **Decorations**, **Trim**, **Filters**, **Transform**, etc.
- Afterward, choose **"Save."**

Share pictures and videos

- Launch the Gallery app.
- Then choose **"Pictures."**
- Proceed by clicking the three vertical dots.
- Then select **"Edit."**
- Go ahead and choose the image/video you intend to share.
- Afterward, choose " ⌁ **Share**."
- Proceed by selecting an application where you intend to share the chosen file.
- Go through the prompts to finish.

Delete pictures and videos

- Launch the Gallery application.
- Afterward, press the three vertical buttons.

- Then choose " ✎ **Edit**."
- Proceed by tapping your desired image(s) or video(s) to choose them.
- Next up, select "**Delete**."

Group similar images

You can sort the media contents in your Gallery application based on how similar they are.

- Launch the Gallery app.

- Then select " ⬚⬚ **Group similar images**."

- To ungroup, press " ⬚⬚ **Ungroup similar images**."

Take a screenshot

By just tapping the buttons on your Galaxy Ultra, you can automatically capture an image on your device's screen.

While on any screen, press and let go of the Side and Volume down button on the body of your Galaxy Ultra.

Palm swipe to capture

You can also capture a screenshot when you swipe the tip of your hand from left to right (and vice versa) on your Galaxy Ultra screen while touching the screen.

- Launch the Settings app.
- From there, hit "**Advanced features**."
- After this, hit "**Motions and gestures**."
- Afterward, hit on "**Palm swipe to capture**."

- Then press to activate it.

Screen recorder

You can film your Galaxy Ultra screen and even share it with anyone.

- Start by opening the notification panel, then swipe down.

- From there, press " **Screen recorder**."
- Go ahead and select any sound setting.
- Afterward, choose "**Start recording**."
- A timer will run before it begins to record. Hit "**Skip countdown**" to commence recording instantly.

- Press ![pen icon] **Draw** to sketch on the display.

- Hit ![pointer icon] **Pointer** to display an icon on your smartphone screen when you're using an S Pen.

- Hit ![person icon] **Selfie video** to embed a film from the front camera.

- To discontinue recording, press ![stop icon] **Stop**.

Chapter Nine

How to use the AI Features

The Galaxy Ultra comes loaded with stunning artificial intelligence features that will enhance the user's experience. All you need to do is navigate to the "Advanced Intelligence" menu in the Settings app to access them. However, ensure you're logged into your Samsung/Google account to get a complete experience.

Set up the Circle to Search feature

This feature shows you data about a photo, text, or object in any application. Rather than searching manually, just long-press your phone's Home button to activate the search. Go ahead and circle the onscreen object with the S Pen (alternatively, use your finger) to view more information. Clicking on the item will show you more information. However, ensure you have an internet connection.

- Head to Settings.
- Then hit "**Display**."
- Afterward, hit the "**Navigation bar**."
- Press the toggle beside the "**Circle to Search**" option to activate it.

How to use Circle to Search

- Long-tap your Galaxy Ultra Home button.
- Proceed by using the S Pen (or your finger) to circle or highlight your desired object/item.
- The internet search will commence once you let go of your S Pen from your phone screen.

How to use the Interpreter app

You can now have your chats with anyone translated in real-time thanks to the Interpreter app.

Setup and use Translation

- Navigate to the Quick settings menu.
- Then hit "**Interpreter.**"

- Proceed by clicking the language you intend to use next to the microphone icon at the lower-left.
- Go ahead and hit the language next to the upper microphone icon to choose the language of the person you'll be having a conversation with. Hit on "Add languages" for additional languages.
- Then select the icon next to "i" at the upper left to switch the upper half of the display towards the speaker.

Interpreter

- Lastly, press the microphone icon designated for you and speak.
- The application will loudly translate your speech and a transcription of your speech in your native language, as well as a textual translation in the other person's language.

Recent translation history

- Launch the Interpreter app.
- Hit on the three vertical dots.
- Next up, choose "**Recents**."
- Proceed by swiping upward to locate the translation you're looking for.
- If you intend to copy the Then hit the Copy icon to copy the transcribed translation or hit the Play symbol to hear the audible translation.

How to use the Note Assist

Samsung has incorporated the Note assist feature into the Note application. It uses AI to translate, summarize, and auto-format your notes.

- Head to the Samsung Notes application.
- Then hit the Create note symbol.

- Proceed by writing your note.
- Afterward, press the **Note assist** symbol just above the keyboard.

- Go ahead and choose from the options (**Translate**, **Summarise**, etc.) that pop up.

How to use Note assist Generate cover

Thanks to the addition of the Generate Cover feature, users can now generate distinctive thumbnail symbols for their notes, making it easier to locate a particular note.

- Navigate to the Samsung Notes app.
- Long-tap a note.
- Then hit the "**More**" button.

- From there, hit "**Generate cover.**"

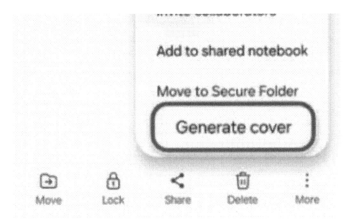

Add to shared notebook

Move to Secure Folder

Generate cover

| Move | Lock | Share | Delete | More |

- Lastly, hit "**Done**."

How to use Generative photo editing

Thanks to AI, the Galaxy Ultra is now able to analyze a photo and recreate it when you crop, delete, or switch the objects in the photo. Also, IT is able to automatically add the ideal background color and even erase items in the photo.

- Head to the Gallery app.
- Go ahead and choose a photograph.
- Hit on the Edit symbol to launch the editing mode.

- Then press the **Generative edit** symbol.

- Proceed by tapping the object or sketch a line around it to choose an object.
- Long-tap on them to remove, reposition, or crop objects.
- Proceed by adjusting the tilt slider to align photos.
- Then hit "**Generate**."

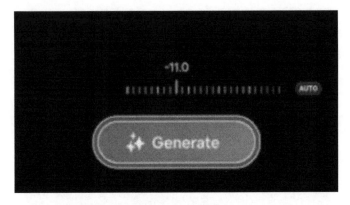

- Afterward, press "**Done**."

How to use Live Translate for phone calls

Thanks to Live Translate, users can now have their phone calls translated in real-time, making communication in different languages easier.

Enable Live Translate

Ensure you enable Live Translate in the Settings application before attempting the phone call.

- Navigate to Settings.
- From there, hit "**Advanced features**."

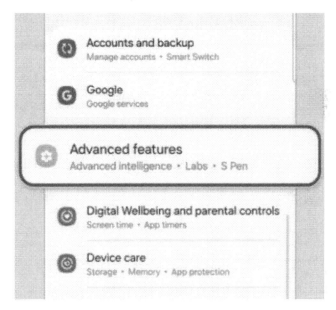

- After this, press "**Advanced intelligence**."

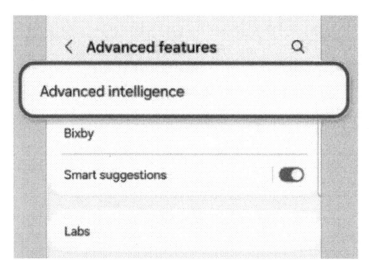

- Then hit on "**Phone**."

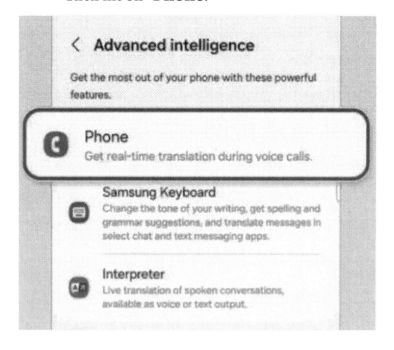

- Press the toggle to set it to **On**. Go through the onscreen guide if a new window appears.

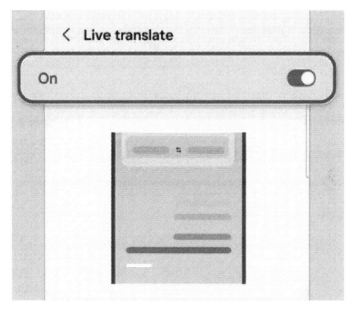

- Proceed by setting your language under the "**Me**" submenu. Then set the language of the person you're speaking with underneath the "**Other person**" submenu.

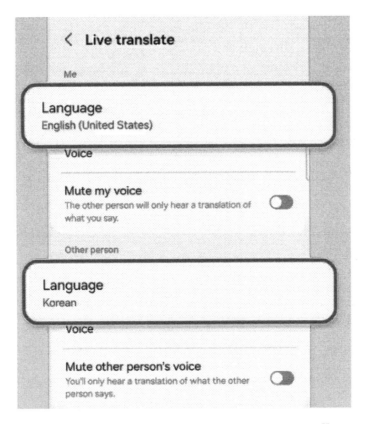

- In some instances, if you have to install the language, hit the download symbol beside the language. After downloading it, move upward, then press the language you require.

Use Live Translate during phone calls

After enabling Live Translate, you can go ahead to try it during a phone call.

- Navigate to the Phone application.

- Go ahead and dial a contact.
- Then hit on **"Call assist."**

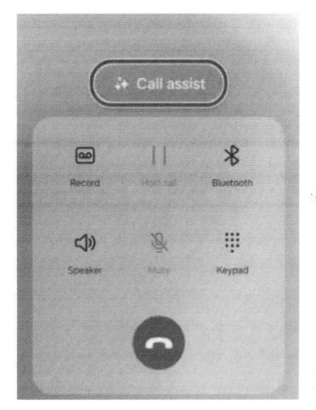

- After this, select **"Live translate."**

How to use Chat translation

The Message application now has a translator tool and can translate your conversations.

Setup Chat translation

- Navigate to Settings.
- After that, press "**Advanced features**."

- Afterward, hit "**Advanced intelligence**."
- Then hit on "**Samsung Keyboard**."

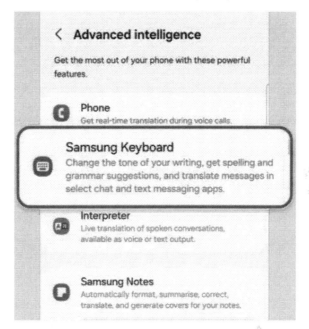

- Next up, hit "**Chat translation**."
- Press the toggle to **On**.

How to use Chat translation

- To use Chat translation, navigate to the Messaging app.
- Then hit the **Writing Assist** symbol.

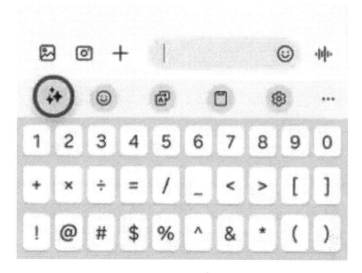

- From there, hit **"Chat translation."**

- Proceed by choosing your desired from the popup. You should see the translated text underneath the original text.

Set up and use the Browsing assist features

When surfing online through the Samsung Internet application, the Browsing Assist can assist you in the translation and summary of texts on a website.

Set up the Summarise feature

The summarization features break down a large chunk of text into the essential points only.

- Head to the Samsung Internet app.
- Then hit the three horizontal lines.
- Afterward, press "**Settings**."

- From there, hit "**Browsing assist**."
- Hit on "**Summarise**."
- Then press the toggle to the "**On**" position.

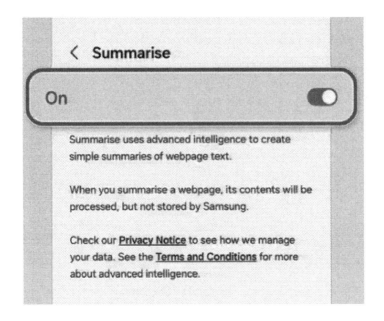

How to use the Summarise feature

- Navigate to the Samsung Internet app.
- Proceed by opening any webpage.
- Afterward, press the **Browsing Assist** symbol.

- Next up, choose "**Summarise**."

How to use the Browsing Assist Translation

- Navigate to the Samsung Internet app.
- Head to any webpage.
- From there, hit the **Browsing Assist** symbol.

- Afterward, press "**Translate**."

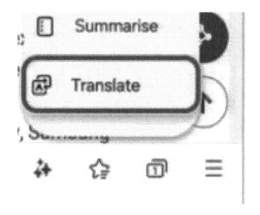

- Go ahead and choose your desired language.
- Lastly, hit "**Translate**."

Chapter Ten

How to Manage Apps

Accessing the App List icon on your Galaxy Ultra will open all the preinstalled and downloaded applications. Also, you can install more applications from the App Store.

To access the app list, swipe upward on your Galaxy Ultra home screen.

Uninstall/Disable Apps

If there are applications you no longer need on your Galaxy Ultra, you can remove or disable them. However, apps that are preinstalled cannot be uninstalled but can be disabled.

- Open your app list, then long-tap an app.
- Next up, choose "**Uninstall**" to delete it from your smartphone, or "**Disable**" to hide it from the app list.

Search for apps

The Search button lets you swiftly locate an application that you're unsure of its location on your phone.

- Open your app list.
- Then select "Search."

- Proceed by entering the app's name.
- Then select the result on your screen to navigate to the app.

Sort apps

You can have your applications arranged in alphabetical order, or you can personalize the order in which they appear.

- Open your app list.
- Then select ⦙.
- Afterward, choose "**Sort**."
- Then select "**Alphabetical order**" to layout the apps alphabetically or "**Custom order**" to manually arrange them.

Create and use folders

Creating folders in your Galaxy Ultra is an easy task; you can even group and store similar applications inside.

- On the application list screen, long-tap an app shortcut.
- Proceed by dragging the application shortcut on top of another application shortcut till it's highlighted.
- Let go of the application shortcut to generate the folder.
- **Folder name**: Give the folder a name.

- ◯ **Palette**: Adjust the color of the folder.

- ✛ **Add apps**: Import applications into the folder.

- Hit ‹ **Back** to exit the folder.

Copy a folder to a Home screen

If desired, you can export a folder to your Galaxy Ultra Home screen.

- Open your app list.
- Then, long-tap on the folder.

- Then choose " ⌂ **Add to Home**."

Delete a folder

Once you remove a folder, the applications stored there will go back to the application list.

- Open your app list.
- Then, long-tap on the folder.

- Afterward, hit " 🗑 **Delete folder**."
- Then follow the prompts.

Install unknown apps

- Navigate to Settings.
- Then, press "**Security and privacy.**"
- From there, hit "**Install unknown apps.**"
- Proceed by clicking on the toggle to authorize installation from an application or webpage.

Chapter Eleven

Manage the Calendar App

With the Calendar application, you can mark important dates, and the app will remind you of the events when the date approaches. You can also link your calendar accounts in one place.

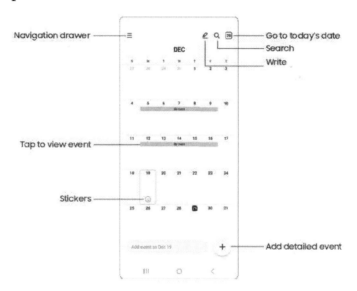

Add calendars

You can import your Calendar accounts to your Galaxy Ultra.

- Launch the Calendar app.

- Then select ▬.

- Afterward, choose "**Manage calendars**."
- From there, select "✛**Add account**."
- Proceed by choosing an account type.
- Go ahead and insert your account details, then go through the prompts.

Calendar alert style

You can personalize the alert style of your Calendar app.

- Launch the Calendar app.
- Then select ☰.

- Afterward, choose ⚙.
- Then hit "**Alert style**."
- Proceed by selecting "**Medium**," "**Strong**" or "**Light**."

Create an event

- Launch the Calendar app.

- Then choose ⊕.
- From Calendar, tap Add detailed event to add an event.
- Proceed by inserting the information of the event.
- Next, choose "**Save**."

Delete an event

- Launch the Calendar app.
- Then choose an event.
- Go ahead and press the event once more to customize it.

- Then choose 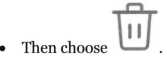 .

Chapter Twelve

How to use the Clock App

With the Clock application, you can add an alarm, timer, and stopwatch, and lookup the time zones of various regions.

Add Alarm

By default, when you open the Clock app, it'll load the Alarm tab. You can add repeating or one-time alarms.

- Launch the Clock app.

- Then choose ✚ .
- Press "**Time**" to add the timer to initiate the alarm.
- Hit "**Day**" to select the alarm date.
- Hit on "**Alarm name**" to insert the alarm name.
- Hit "**Vibration**" to select if the alarm will vibrate.
- Press "**Alarm sound**" to select a sound for the alarm.
- Then choose "**Save**."

Delete an alarm

- Launch the Clock app.
- Long-tap the alarm.

- Then press  .

Alarm settings

In the Alarm settings menu, you can make your smartphone send alerts for upcoming alarms.

- Launch the Clock app.
- Then choose ⋮ .
- Afterward, select "**Settings**."
- From there, hit "**Upcoming alarm notification**."
- Proceed y selecting the duration before an upcoming alarm.

Add Stopwatch

If you're thinking of timing an event, the Stopwatch tab in the Clock app will come in handy.

- Launch the Clock app.
- Then select the "**Stopwatch**" tab.
- Afterward, hit "Start" to commence timing.
- Hit "**Lap**" to monitor lap times.
- To discontinue timing, hit "**Stop**."

- Hit "**Resume**" if you desire to resume timing after you've stopped the clock.
- To reset, hit "**Reset**."

Add Timer

The Timer tab in the Clock application will let you add a countdown timer to your desired hours, minutes, and seconds.

- Launch the Clock app.
- Then select the "**Timer**" tab.
- Proceed by clicking "**Minutes**," "**Seconds**" & "**Hours**" to configure the Timer.
- To commence the timer, press "**Start**."
- To pause, hit "**Pause**."
- To continue after pausing the timer, press "**Resume**."
- Hit "**Delete**" if you intend to discontinue and reset the Timer.

Preset timer

You can label and also save customized timers.

- Launch the Clock app.
- Then select the "**Timer**" tab.
- Then select ⦙.
- Afterward, hit "**Add preset timer**."
- Proceed by setting the countdown time, then insert the timer's name.

- Then choose "**Add**."
- If you need to customize any saved

   preset timer, press ⦙ , then hit "**Edit preset timers**."

Timer options

The Timer has a settings menu where you can adjust its sound and other settings.

- Launch the Clock app.
- Then select the "**Timer**" tab.
- Then select the three vertical dots.
- Afterward, press "**Settings**."
- Proceed by tapping "**Vibration**," "**Show mini timer**," or "**Sound**" to edit.

Chapter Thirteen

Manage Contacts

Having all your contacts in one place is a great deal. With your Galaxy Ultra, you can manage and save your contacts and even import them from your email accounts.

Create a contact

Saving a contact on your Galaxy Ultra is easy.

- Launch the Contacts app.

- Then hit the plus button ✛.
- Proceed by inserting the contact's information.
- Afterward, choose "**Save.**"

Edit a contact

You can modify information about any contact that is stored in your Galaxy Ultra.

- Launch the Contacts app.
- Then select a contact.

- Next, choose "✏ **Edit.**"
- Proceed by clicking on any of the fields to make your changes.
- Then select "**Save.**"

Favorites

By marking a contact as a favorite, it'll display at the top of your contact list.

- Launch the Contacts app.
- Then select a contact.

- Afterward, press .

- Hit to erase the contact from Favorites.

Share a contact

- Launch the Contacts app.
- Then select a contact.

- Afterward, choose .
- Proceed by tapping "**Text**" or "**vCard file (VCF).**"
- Go ahead and select your desired sharing method.

Display contacts when sharing Files

If you would rather have your contacts pop up whenever you want to share media content or an app, you can set your phone to display your favorite contacts on the Share menu.

- Launch the Settings app.
- From there, hit "**Advanced features**."
- Proceed by tapping "**Show contacts when sharing content**."

- Then press the toggle ⬤ to activate it.

Create a group

You can organize your contacts into groups such as Work, School, etc.

- Launch the Contacts app.

- Hit on ☰.
- Then choose "**Groups**."
- From there, hit "**Create group**."
- Proceed by clicking the fields to insert the group information.
- Afterward, choose "**Save**."

Add group contacts

- Launch the Contacts app.

- Next, choose " ✎ **Edit**."
- Then select "**Add member**."
- Proceed by selecting the contacts you desire to add.
- Next, choose "**Save**."

Remove group contacts

- Launch the Contacts app.
- Hit on ▦.
- Then choose "**Groups**."
- Go ahead and choose a group.
- Long-tap the contact to choose it.
- Afterward, hit "**Remove**."

Send a message to a group

You can compose a text that will be forwarded to all contacts in a group.

- Launch the Contacts app.
- Hit on ▦.
- Then choose "**Groups**."
- Proceed by selecting a group.
- Hit on the triple vertical dots.
- Then choose "**Send message**."

Delete a group

- Launch the Contacts app.
- Hit on ▦.
- Then choose "**Groups**."
- Proceed by selecting a group.
- Hit on the triple vertical dots.
- Next, hit "**Delete group**."

- If you only need to remove the group, hit "**Delete group only**." However, if you need to remove the group as well as the contacts that are stored within it, hit "**Delete group and move members to the trash**."

Merge contacts

You can merge contact details with duplicate information into one by connecting their entries.

- Launch the Contacts app.
- Hit on ▬.
- Then choose "**Manage contacts**."
- Afterward, hit "**Merge contacts**."
- Go ahead and choose the contacts.
- Then select "**Merge**."

Import contacts

- Launch the Contacts app.
- Hit on ▬.
- From there, hit "**Manage contacts**."
- After this, hit "**Import contacts**."

Export contacts

- Launch the Contacts app.

- Hit on 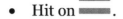.
- Next, press "**Manage contacts**."
- Up next, press "**Export contacts**."

Sync contacts

Syncing your contacts enables you to have them updated across all your accounts.

- Launch the Contacts app.
- Hit on .
- Now, hit "**Manage contacts**."
- Afterward, hit "**Sync contacts**."

Delete contacts

- Launch the Contacts app.
- Long-tap a contact. To delete multiple contacts, click to choose them.
- Then hit 🗑.

Emergency contacts

You can choose a contact as your emergency contact. This person will be alerted whenever you have an emergency. They can even be contacted when your smartphone is locked.

- Launch the Settings app.

- From there, hit **"Safety and emergency."**
- Afterward, hit **"Emergency contacts."**
- Hit on **"Add member"** to select the contact that will be alerted during emergencies.
- Hit on **"Show on Lock screen"** to have your emergency contact(s) displayed on your Galaxy Ultra lock screen for easy access.

Chapter Fourteen

Internet App

The default browser on the Galaxy Ultra is the Samsung Internet browser. It works just like any browser. However, some beginners might have a hard time; that's why the tips here will come in handy.

Browser tabs

The browser tabs let you see different webpages simultaneously.

- Launch the Internet app.

- Then hit the Tabs button 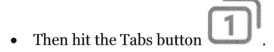.

- Afterward, select "**New tab**."

- If you need to exit a tab, press ,

  then hit .

Create a Bookmark

By bookmarking your regular websites, you can swiftly open them.

- Launch the Internet app.

- Then choose the bookmark icon to save it.

Open a Bookmark

- Launch the Internet app.

- Then choose .
- Go ahead and click a bookmark entry.

View history

You can access your recently viewed websites by navigating to the History menu.

- Launch the Internet app.

- Then select .

- Afterward, press "**History**."
- If you need to wipe off your browsing history, press the triple vertical dots icon, then select "**Clear history**."

Share pages
- Launch the Internet app.
- Then select ▬▬.
- Afterward, press "**Share**."

Secret mode
When you browse in secret mode, your browsing history will not show the websites you visit, and your device will not store any cookies. It is called private mode on some devices.

- Launch the Internet app.
- Then select ⬛.
- Proceed by tapping "**Turn on Secret mode**."
- After this, hit "**Start**" to commence surfing the internet in private mode.

Turn off Secret mode
- Launch the Internet app.

- Now, hit  .
- Next, hit **"Turn off Secret mode."**

Internet settings

You can also adjust other internet settings through its Settings menu.

- Launch the Internet app.
- Next, hit ▬▬ .
- Then press **"Settings."**

Chapter Fifteen

Manage the Phone App

The Phone application lets you manage your calls, including how to navigate some advanced features.

Make a call

With the Phone app, you can dial a number that isn't stored on your Contacts list.

- Launch the Phone app.
- Proceed by inserting the number you intend to dial through the keypad. If the keypad doesn't pop up, press **"Keypad."**
- Then hit "  **Call**."

Make a call from Contacts

Rather than using the Phone app, you can decide to call someone through the Contacts app.

- Launch the Contacts app.
- Proceed by swiping your finger over a contact to the right.

Answer a call

Once you have an incoming call, your Galaxy Ultra will ring and you should see the call pop up on the display.

- To answer an incoming call while on the call screen, go ahead and drag the " Answer" button towards the right.
- To answer the call on the pop-up screen, press " Answer."

Decline a call

If you don't wish to answer an incoming call, you can decline it. This will forward the call to your voicemail.

- On call screen: Proceed by dragging the " Decline" button towards the left.

- Pop-up screen: Press " Decline."

End a call

If you answered the call and choose to end it,

press "  **End call**."

Call background

You can choose an image or video that will display whenever you're making or receiving a phone call.

- Launch the Phone app.
- Then select the triple vertical dots.
- Hit on "**Settings**."
- Then press "**Call background**."
- Proceed by selecting "**Layout**" and "**Background**" to customize.

Call log

Your call logs contain the numbers you've dialed and the calls you've received or missed.

- Launch the Phone app.
- Then select "**Recents**."

Save a contact from a recent call

If you recently talked with someone over the phone and wish to save their number, the process is easy.

- Launch the Phone app.
- Then select "**Recents**."
- Go ahead and select the call, then hit "**Add to contacts**."
- Proceed by tapping "**Create new contact**." Alternatively, hit "**Update existing contact**."

Delete call records

- Launch the Phone app.
- Then select "**Recents**."
- Long-tap the call you desire to remove from your Call log.

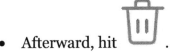

- Afterward, hit   .

Block a number

After adding someone to the block list, their calls will be forwarded to your voicemail, and you'll not get any messages from them.

- Launch the Phone app.
- Then select "**Recents**."
- Go ahead and click the contact.

- Afterward, select " ⓘ **Details**."
- Press the triple vertical dots icon.
- Then hit "**Block contact**."

Place a multi-party call

You can call another person while on an ongoing call and then merge both calls or switch between them.

- While you're on an active call, hit ✛ to call the second contact.
- Then insert the phone number and hit "

   Call."
- Once the person answers the call, press "

  ↱ **Swap**" to alternate between both

  calls or "⤳ **Merge**" for a conference call.

Video calls

You can make video calls directly from the Phone app.

- Launch the Phone app.
- Go ahead and insert the number.
- Afterward, press "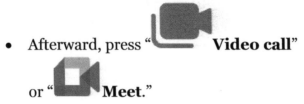**Video call**" or "**Meet**."

Wi-Fi calling

You can even make calls when your Galaxy Ultra is paired with a Wi-Fi network.

- Launch the Phone app.
- Afterward, press the triple vertical dots icon.
- Hit on "**Settings**."
- Then press "**Wi-Fi calling**."
- Next, press ⬤ to activate this feature.
- Go through the prompts to configure the settings.

Real-Time Text (RTT)

During a phone call, you can send and text from the person you're talking with over the phone if their device supports RTT. Real-time chat is also possible if they have their smartphone paired with a teletypewriter (TTY) gadget.

- Launch the Phone app.
- Then hit the triple vertical dots icon.
- Hit on "**Settings**."
- Afterward, choose "**Real time text**."
- Go ahead and select from the displayed options.

Set up Voicemail

Your voicemails can be accessed via the Phone app and you can configure it when desired.

- Launch the Phone app .
- Long-tap the " **1 key**" or press "
Voicemail."
- Go through the prompt to finish.

Samsung Notes App

Galaxy Ultra users can use the Samsung Notes application to do voice recordings and make notes that contain texts, pictures, and audio that can be shared with anyone.

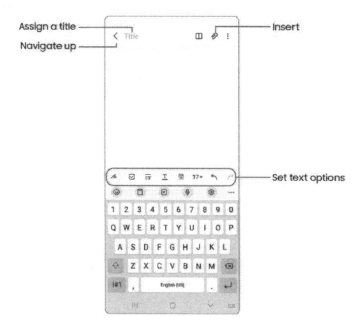

Assign a title

Navigate up

Insert

Set text options

Create notes

Making notes on the Samsung Notes application is simple.

- Launch the Samsung Notes app.

- Then hit .

- Proceed by using the text options to make your notes.

Voice recordings

- Launch the Samsung Notes app.

- Then hit .

- Afterward, press .
- Now, hit "**Voice recording**."
- Proceed by using the text options to make your recording.

Edit notes

After creating a note, you can customize it.

- Launch the Samsung Notes.
- Then choose a note to open it.

- Afterward, hit .
- Proceed to make the changes.

- After that, press ‹ .

Chapter Sixteen

How to Manage Connections

The Connection menu in the Settings app lets you manage your Galaxy Ultra connection with other devices, Bluetooth, Wi-Fi networks, and more.

Set up Wi-Fi

Rather than accessing the internet with mobile data, you can do that by pairing your Galaxy Ultra with a Wi-Fi network.

- Launch the Settings app.
- Then hit "**Connections**."
- After this, press "**Wi-Fi**."
- Proceed by tapping on the toggle button to activate Wi-Fi. Your smartphone will start scanning for available networks.
- Go ahead and choose a network.
- Afterward, insert the network's password, if needed.
- Next, hit "**Connect**."

Enable Wi-Fi Direct

With Wi-Fi Direct, users can transfer data wirelessly across different devices.

- Launch the Settings app.
- From there, hit "**Connections**."
- Afterward, hit "**Wi-Fi**."
- Press the toggle to activate Wi-Fi.
- Then select ⦂.
- From there, choose "**Wi-Fi Direct**."
- Proceed by clicking on a device.
- Go through the prompts to pair.

Disconnect from Wi-Fi Direct

- Launch the Settings app.
- Then press "**Connections**."
- Afterward, hit "**Wi-Fi**."
- Then select ⦂.
- After this, hit "**Wi-Fi Direct**."
- Go ahead and choose a device to unpair it.

Enable Bluetooth

You can transfer and receive media contents and files from other smartphone users through Bluetooth.

- Launch the Settings app.

- Then press "**Connections**."
- Afterward, hit "**Bluetooth**."
- Press the toggle button to activate Bluetooth.
- Proceed by choosing a device, then go through the prompts to pair.

Rename a paired device

- Launch the Settings app.
- Afterward, hit "**Connections**."
- From there, hit "**Bluetooth**."
- Proceed by pressing the toggle button to activate Bluetooth.
- Then press the cogwheel icon by the side of the device's name.
- Next, hit "**Rename**."
- Go ahead and insert a new name.
- Afterward, hit "**Rename**."

Unpair from a Bluetooth device

Once you unpair any device from Bluetooth, that device will be unable to automatically recognize your Galaxy Ultra until you pair it again.

- Launch the Settings app.
- Next up, hit "**Connections**."
- Afterward, press "**Bluetooth**."

- Proceed by pressing the toggle button to activate Bluetooth.
- After this, hit the cogwheel icon beside the device's name.
- Then hit "**Unpair**."
- Now, choose "**Unpair**" to finish.

NFC and payment

NFC, which stands for "Near Field Communication," enables your Galaxy Ultra to exchange data wirelessly with another device by pairing both devices. The technology is mostly used to make contactless payments.

- Launch the Settings app.
- Next up, hit "**Connections**."
- After this, hit "**NFC and contactless payments**."
- Proceed by pressing the toggle button to activate NFC.

Enable Tap and pay

With an NFC payment application, users can make payments by placing their Galaxy Ultra on top of a supported credit card terminal.

- Launch the Settings app.
- From there, press "**Connections**."

- After that, press "**NFC and contactless payments**."
- Proceed by clicking the toggle button  to activate NFC.
- Hit on "**Contactless payments**" to launch your default payment application.
- If you desire to utilize a different payment app, click the application to select it.

Enable Airplane mode

Once you activate Airplane mode on your Galaxy Ultra, it'll disable all your network connections. However, you can still enable Wi-Fi and Bluetooth.

- Launch the Settings app.
- Next up, hit "**Connections**."
- Afterward, hit "**Airplane mode**."
- Go ahead and press the toggle button to activate Airplane mode.

View Data usage

You can see your mobile and Wi-Fi data consumption as well as edit warnings and limits.

- Launch the Settings app.
- After this, press "**Connections**."
- Afterward, hit "**Data usage**."

Turn on the Data saver

You can cut down on your data usage by disabling the transfer and receiving of data in the background.

- Launch the Settings app.
- From there, hit "**Connections**."
- Next up, press "**Data usage**."
- Afterward, hit "**Data saver**."
- Go ahead and press the toggle button to activate the Data saver.

Add Mobile hotspot

You can allow other devices to connect to your Galaxy Ultra and use your phone's data plan thanks to a mobile hotspot.

- Launch the Settings app.
- Then, hit "**Connections**."

- After this, press "**Mobile hotspot and tethering.**"
- From there, hit "**Mobile hotspot.**"
- Next up, press the toggle to activate the Mobile hotspot.
- Take out the device you desire to pair and enable Wi-Fi. Go ahead and choose your Galaxy Ultra Mobile hotspot.
- Proceed by inserting the mobile hotspot password to pair.
- All the paired devices will be displayed underneath the "**Connected devices**" section.

Enable Auto hotspot

Auto hotspot allows other device(s) that are logged into your Samsung account to automatically pair with your hotspot connection.

- Launch the Settings app.
- Then, hit "**Connections.**"
- After this, press "**Mobile hotspot and tethering.**"
- From there, hit "**Mobile hotspot.**"
- Next up, choose "**Auto hotspot.**"
- Then press the toggle button to activate it.

Set up Tethering

With tethering, users can share the internet connection of their Galaxy Ultra with other devices.

- Launch the Settings app.
- Then, hit "**Connections**."
- After this, press "**Mobile hotspot and tethering**."
- Proceed by tapping an option. Choose "**Bluetooth tethering**" to use Bluetooth for sharing your smartphone's internet connection.
- Use a USB cable to connect your PC and smartphone, then hit "**USB tethering**."
- If you're connecting your PC to a Galaxy Ultra through an Ethernet adapter, then hit "**Ethernet tethering**."

Nearby device scanning

Nearby device scanning lets you comfortably configure connections to other available gadgets.

- Launch the Settings app.
- Then, hit "**Connections**."
- After this, press "**More connection settings**."
- From there, hit "**Nearby device scanning**."

- Proceed by pressing the toggle button to activate the feature.

Connect to a printer

If you need to print files through your Galaxy Ultra, ensure your phone and the printer are paired to the Wi-Fi network.

- Launch the Settings app.
- Then, hit "**Connections**."
- Next up, hit "**More connection settings**."
- After that, press "**Printing**."
- Go ahead and hit "**Default print service**."

- Afterward, hit ⦂.
- Next up, press "**Add printer**."
- Some printers will need a plugin, just hit on "Download plugin," then go through the guide to register a print service.

Virtual Private Networks

VPN lets users encrypt their smartphones by connecting them to a secret, secured network.

- Launch the Settings app.
- Then, hit "**Connections**."

- From there, hit "**More connection settings**."
- After this, hit "**VPN**."
- Then hit the three vertical dots.
- Afterward, hit "**Add VPN profile**."
- Proceed by inserting the VPN network details given by your network administrator.
- After that, hit "**Save**."

Manage a VPN

You can personalize or remove a VPN connection.

- Launch the Settings app.
- Then, hit "**Connections**."
- Next up, press "**More connection settings**."
- Afterward, select "**VPN**."
- Go ahead and press the cogwheel icon next to a VPN.
- Proceed by editing the VPN, then select "**Save**." To remove it, hit "**Delete**."

Connect to a VPN

- Launch the Settings app.
- Then, hit "**Connections**."
- Afterward, choose "**More connection settings**."
- From there, hit "**VPN**."

- Go ahead and choose a VPN.
- Proceed by entering your sign-in credentials, then hit "**Connect**."
- If you need to disconnect, press "**Disconnect**."

Enable Private DNS

The Galaxy Ultra also lets you pair your phone with a private DNS host.

- Launch the Settings app.
- Then, hit "**Connections**."
- Next up, hit "**More connection settings**."
- From there, hit "**Private DNS**."
- Proceed by selecting an option to set it up.
- Afterward, hit "**Save**."

Add Ethernet

If you're unable to pair with a wireless network connection, try using an Ethernet cable to link your Galaxy Ultra to a local network.

- Launch the Settings app.
- Then, hit "**Connections**."
- Afterward, press "**More connection settings**."
- Next up, hit "**Ethernet**."

- Go through the prompts.

Chapter Seventeen

Sounds and Vibration

Managing the sound and vibration of your Galaxy Ultra is something you'll definitely have to do at some point.

Choose Sound mode

In the Sounds and Vibration menu of the Settings app, you can adjust the sound mode of your Galaxy Ultra.

- Launch the Settings app.
- Then, hit "**Sounds and vibration.**"
- Proceed by tapping a mode (Sound, Mute, Vibrate, etc.) to select and customize it.

Mute with gestures

To swiftly silence your smartphone's sound, just turn it over or cover the display.

- Launch the Settings app.
- Then, hit "**Advanced features.**"
- Afterward, hit on "**Motions and gestures.**"
- Go ahead and press "**Mute with gestures.**"
- Hit the toggle to activate it.

Adjust Phone Volume

The Settings menu offers an alternative way to adjust the volume of your Galaxy Ultra if you do not wish to use the volume key.

- Launch the Settings app.
- Then, hit "**Sounds and vibration**."
- Afterward, hit on "**Volume**."
- Proceed by dragging the slider for your preferred sound type.

Add Ringtone

Your Galaxy Ultra comes with some preinstalled ringtones that you can select or personalize. Also, you can add your own desired sound as your ringtone.

- Launch the Settings app.
- Next up, press "**Sounds and vibration**."
- After that, hit "**Ringtone**."
- Proceed by dragging the slider to modify your ringtone volume.
- Click on a ringtone to listen to it, then choose it. Or, press the plus button to save it as your ringtone.

Adjust Notification sound

You can select the sound for the notifications that you get on your Galaxy Ultra.

- Launch the Settings app.
- Afterward, hit "**Sounds and vibration**."
- From there, hit "**Notification sound**."
- Proceed by dragging the slider to modify the sound volume of the notifications.
- Click on a sound to listen to it, then choose it.

Enable Dolby Atmos

You can experience the Dolby Atmos quality on your Galaxy Ultra once you're using a headphone.

- Launch the Settings app.
- Afterward, hit "**Sounds and vibration**."
- From there, press "**Sound quality and effects**."
- Then hit and enable "**Dolby Atmos**."

Add Equalizer

You can select an audio setup suited to various categories of music or do it manually.

- Launch the Settings app.

- Next up, hit "**Sounds and vibration**."
- After this, hit "**Sound quality and effects**."
- Proceed by choosing "**Equalizer**" to pick your music category.

Add UHQ upscaler

UHQ upscaler helps boost the audio and video quality to provide a better experience. It only works when you're putting on a headphone.

- Launch the Settings app.
- Now, press "**Sounds and vibration**."
- From there, hit "**Sound quality and effects**."
- Go ahead and hit "**UHQ upscaler**."
- Then select your desired upscaling option.

Choose App notifications

You can edit the applications that you want to get alerts from.

- Launch the Settings app.
- Now, press "**Notifications**."
- From there, hit "**App notifications**."
- Go ahead and press the toggle button to activate notifications for each application.

Lock screen notifications

You can modify the notifications that will pop up on your Galaxy Ultra Lock screen.

- Launch the Settings app.
- Next, hit "**Notifications**."
- After that, hit "**Lock screen notifications**."
- Proceed by tapping the toggle button to activate it.
- Go ahead and choose an option to edit it.

Notification pop-up style

You can adjust how your notifications appear on your device screen.

- Launch the Settings app.
- From there, choose "**Notifications**."
- Afterward, hit on "**Notification pop-up style**."
- Proceed by selecting a pop-up style.

Enable Do not disturb

Do not disturb, which is written as "DND" for short; lets you prevent your Galaxy Ultra from sending alerts or sounds when the mode is activated. However, you can make exemptions for some contacts, applications, and alarms.

- Launch the Settings app.
- From there, choose "**Notifications**."
- Afterward, hit on "**Do not disturb**" to configure it.
- Then hit "**For how long?**" to select the duration.

Alert when phone picked up

You can set your Galaxy Ultra to always vibrate whenever you pick it up, in case you've missed calls and messages.

- Launch the Settings app.
- Next, hit "**Advanced features**."
- After that, hit "**Motions and gestures**."
- From there, hit "**Alert when phone picked**."

Chapter Eighteen

Manage the Display Settings

You can adjust the font, screen, timeout, and various display settings of your Galaxy Ultra.

Enable Dark mode

For a darker theme on your Galaxy Ultra, you should activate Dark mode.

- Launch the Settings app.
- Next, hit "**Display**."
- After that, hit "**Motions and gestures**."
- From there, hit "**Dark**." You can select when Dark mode is applied.
- Hit "**Turn on as scheduled**" and select "**Sunset to sunrise**" to apply the dark theme from night till the next morning or "**Custom schedule**" to manually personalize the duration.

Enable Screen brightness

- Launch the Settings app.
- Next, hit "**Display**."

- Proceed by dragging the Brightness slider underneath the **"Brightness"** menu to adjust it.
- To automatically modify the screen brightness according to the ambient condition, press **"Adaptive brightness."**

Enable Motion smoothness

You can make the scrolling your smartphone faster.

- Launch the Settings app.
- Next, hit **"Display."**
- Afterward, hit **"Motion smoothness."**
- Go ahead and choose an option.
- Next up, hit **"Apply."**

Enable Eye comfort shield

Spending too much time on the screen can cause eye strain. You can reduce that by turning on the Eye Comfort Shield on your Galaxy Ultra.

- Launch the Settings app.
- Next, hit **"Display."**

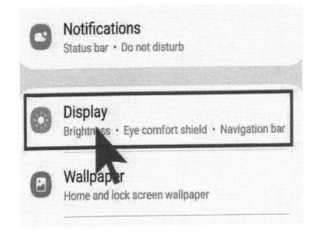

- Afterward, hit "**Eye comfort shield.**"

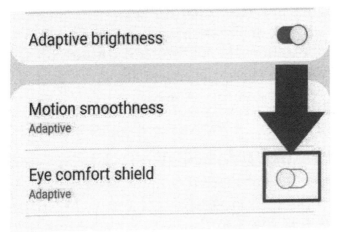

- Go ahead and press to activate it.
- Choose an option to personalize it.

Change Screen mode

You can select different screen modes, which let you customize the screen quality depending on the purpose.

- Launch the Settings app.
- Next, hit "**Display**."
- Afterward, hit "**Screen mode**."
- Proceed by clicking an option to apply another screen mode. You can push the slider to change the white balance.

Adjust Font size and style

- Launch the Settings app.
- Next, hit "**Display**."
- Afterward, hit "**Font size and style**."
- To pick another font, hit "**Font style**." Then click on a font to choose it.

  Alternately, hit ✚ to install fonts from the app store.
- For bold fonts, hit "**Bold font**."
- Then push the slider to personalize the text size.

Enable Screen Zoom

You can change the zoom of your smartphone to make the content more legible.

- Launch the Settings app.
- Then, press "**Display**."
- After this, hit "**Screen Zoom**."
- Proceed by dragging the slider to modify the zoom level.

Change Screen resolution

You can enhance your Galaxy Ultra screen resolution for sharper image quality or reduce it to conserve your phone battery.

- Launch the Settings app.
- Then, press "**Display**."
- After this, hit "**Screen resolution**."
- Go ahead and hit on your desired resolution.
- Then hit "**Apply**."

Add Camera cutout

Your Galaxy Ultra can mask its camera cutout section with a black strip.

- Launch the Settings app.
- Then, press "**Display**."
- After this, hit "**Camera cutout**."
- Proceed by selecting applications to activate the Camera cutout, then personalize the options.

Add Screen timeout

You can make your Galaxy Ultra screen go off after a set duration of inactivity.

- Launch the Settings app.
- Then, press "**Display**."
- After this, hit "**Screen timeout**."
- Go ahead and choose a time limit.

Enable Accidental touch protection

You can set your smartphone not to detect touch input whenever it is placed somewhere dark like your pocket.

- Launch the Settings app.
- From there, hit "**Display**."
- Afterward, hit "**Accidental touch protection**."

Enable Touch sensitivity

You can make your Galaxy Ultra screen more sensitive to touches, especially when using a screen protector.

- Launch the Settings app.
- From there, hit "**Display**."
- Lastly, hit "**Touch sensitivity**."

Enable Lift to wake

You can make your Galaxy Ultra turn on automatically whenever you raise it.

- Launch the Settings app.
- After this, "**Advanced features**."
- From there, hit "**Motions and gestures**."
- Then, hit "**Lift to wake**."

Double-tap to turn on screen

You can turn on your Galaxy Ultra display by tapping it twice.

- Launch the Settings app.
- Afterward, select "**Advanced features**."
- Next up, press "**Motions and gestures**."
- Lastly, hit "**Double tap**."

Multi-window

Samsung has a feature for multitaskers that allows them to use multiple applications simultaneously, and they can easily switch between applications and change their size as well.

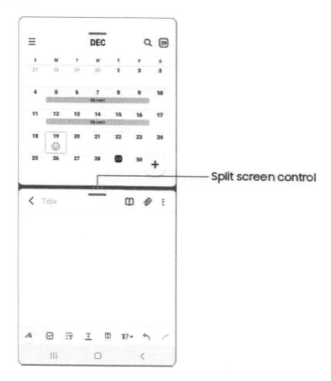

Split screen control

- Press ||| on your Galaxy Ultra.
- Then choose the application icon.
- Next up, touch "**Open in split screen view**."
- Proceed by clicking on an application in the other window to include it in the split screen mode.
- Follow up by dragging the center of the window border to change the size of the window.

Window controls

You can adjust how the application windows appear in split screen mode.

Begin by dragging the center of the window border to change the dimension of the windows.

Then press the center of the window border; some options will appear:

Add app pair to ☆ : This option will generate and add an application pair shortcut.

Switch window ↑↓: This option enables you to swap both windows.

Edge panels

The Edge panels offer a faster way of accessing your favorite applications. To view the shortcut items in the Edge Panel, all you need to do is drag the Edge Panel handle to the left to view them.

- Launch the Settings app.
- Then hit "**Display**."
- From there, choose "**Edge panels**."
- Then press  to activate Edge panels.

Change the Edge panels

You can customize the Edge Panels to only show the items you want.

- Launch the Settings app.
- Then hit "**Display**."
- Then choose "**Edge panels**."
- From there, choose "**Panels**."
- Proceed by choosing the tab panel you prefer to use.

Apps panel

Depending on your preference, you can include some applications in the Apps panel.

Begin by dragging the Edge handle to the middle of the display.

Follow up by swiping until the Apps panel pops up.

Go ahead and click on an application or applications pair shortcut to access it.

Alternatively, press "⦂⦂⦂ **All apps**" to load the complete list.

Customize App panel

- If you need to personalize the Apps panel, begin by dragging the Edge handle to the middle of the display. Keep swiping until the Apps panel pops up.

- To include other applications in the Apps panel, hit "**Edit**." Locate the app and click it to have it added to the available space.
- If you need to set up a folder shortcut, start by dragging an application from the left and drop it on another application on the right.
- To rearrange the applications, drag each application to your preferred position.
- To delete an application, press "**Remove**."

Chapter Nineteen

Factory Data Reset

A factory data reset erases all your device files and data, and your settings will return to default. Before attempting a factory reset, ensure you've backed up your data.

- Head to the Settings app.
- From there, choose "**General management**."
- Afterward, hit "**Reset**."
- Next up, hit "**Factory data reset**."
- From there, hit "**Reset**."
- Go through the guide to reset your smartphone.

TalkBack

TalkBack is an accessibility feature that lets users navigate their Galaxy Ultra without having to look at the display.

- Head to the Settings app.
- After this, hit "**Accessibility**."
- Then select "**TalkBack**."
- Press to activate it.

- Go ahead and hit "**TalkBack shortcut**" or "**Settings**" to customize the TalkBack settings.

Spoken assistance

Spoken assistance uses special controls and works similarly to the TalkBack features.

- Head to the Settings app.
- After this, hit "**Accessibility**."
- From there, select "**Spoken assistance**."

- Hit on to activate it.
- Go ahead and select an option to personalize it.

Visibility enhancements

You can also personalize the color and contrasts to enhance your visual experience.

- Head to the Settings app.
- After this, hit "**Accessibility**."
- Then, hit "**Visibility enhancements**."

- Proceed by selecting an option (Color filter, Default, Large display, etc.), then choose "**Apply**."

Enter text

You can compose text on your Galaxy Ultra by using your voice or keyboard. Also, you can translate and send emojis, among other things.

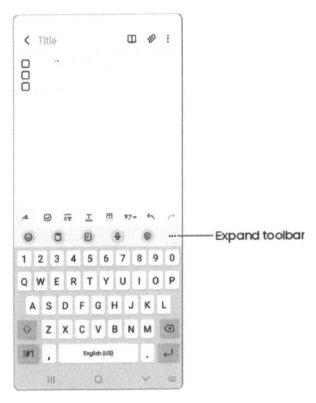

Expand toolbar

For more options, press the "Expand toolbar button and select your desired options such as Voice input, Clipboard, Translate, Handwriting, Grammarly, etc.

Use Samsung voice input

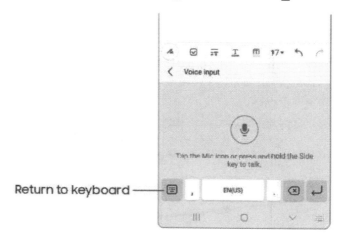

Rather than typing, you can compose text by speaking.

After you've opened the Samsung keyboard,

press the 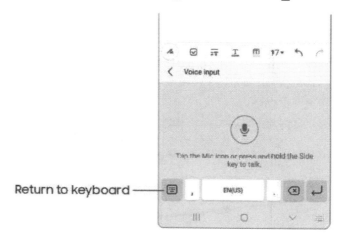 Voice input button, then speak.

Turn on Find My Mobile

This feature helps to track your stolen smartphone by remotely locating, locking, and encrypting it once you're logged into your Samsung account.

- Launch the Settings app.
- Now, hit **"Security and privacy**."
- After that, press **"Find My Mobile**."
- From there, hit **"Allow this phone to be found**."
- Hit the toggle to activate Find My Mobile.
- Proceed by signing into your Samsung account on the Samsung webpage, then choose **"Remote unlock"** to add a screen lock remotely.
- Hit on **"Send last location"** to access the last known location of the smartphone. Select other options to customize.

Chapter Twenty

Digital well-being and parental controls

The Digital Wellbeing menu enables users to track the duration they spend using their smartphone every day, how often they use certain applications, the number of notifications they get, the frequency with which they check their device, and more.

Set a Screen time goal

By setting a screen time goal, you can keep tabs on the duration you spend on your smartphone.

- Launch the Settings app.
- From there, hit "**Digital Wellbeing and parental controls**."
- Underneath "**Screen time goal**," hit on "**Set goal**."

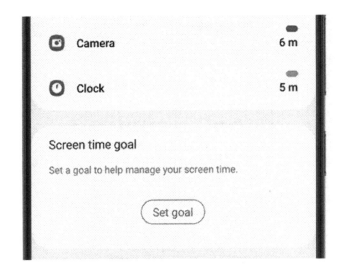

- Proceed by selecting your preferred screen time goal duration.
- Next, hit "**Done.**"
- To access your current usage after creating the schedule, hit on the "**Screen time goal**" tracker, then choose any day of your choice to access your current usage. From here, you'll be able to view the duration you have spent on your Galaxy Ultra for that day.
- If you need to adjust or remove the goal, hit on the three vertical dots, then pick your preferred option.

Set and use app timers

The App Timers menu in the Digital Wellbeing settings screen enables you to keep tabs on the duration you've been using the applications on your Galaxy Ultra, including how many

164

notifications you have received, the duration you've spent on the applications, and how often you've unlocked your device.

- Launch the Settings app.
- From there, hit "**Digital Wellbeing and parental controls**."
- After this, choose "**App timers**."
- Proceed by choosing your preferred applications. Or, press "**All**" at the upper left edge to choose everything.
- Then hit "**Set timer**."
- Go ahead and pick the minutes, days, and hours.
- Afterward, hit "**Done**."

Use Sleep mode

Staring at your phone for a few minutes before bedtime can ruin your sleep. To avoid this, enable sleep mode so that your Galaxy Ultra screen will change to grayscale. This will inform your brain that bedtime is getting close.

- Launch the Settings app.
- Afterward, hit "**Modes and Routines**."
- Then choose "**Sleep**."
- Now, choose "**Start**."
- Proceed by setting your bedtime and wake-up times.
- Then choose "**Next**."

- Proceed by choosing your preferred configuration for App notifications, including for Calls and messages.
- Note: By default, this will enable Do not disturb. To toggle it off, press its switch. Now, hit "**Next**."

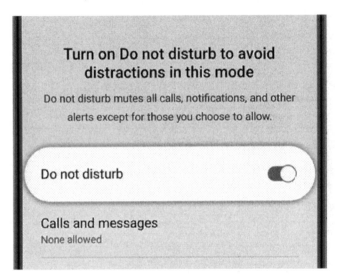

- Also, you can tap settings such as Eye comfort shield, Grayscale, Dark mode, etc., to customize them.
- Once you're finished, hit "**Done**"
- Next up, hit "**Turn on**" to toggle on Sleep mode immediately.

Use Volume monitor

Volume monitor can inform you when music is too loud for your ear if you're wearing headphones or Galaxy Buds.

- Launch the Settings app.
- Afterward, hit "**Digital Wellbeing and parental controls**."
- From there, hit "**Volume monitor**."
- Then choose "**Start**."
- Hit on the three vertical dots.
- Afterward, hit "**Use volume monitor**."
  proceed by pressing the toggle at the top to activate it.

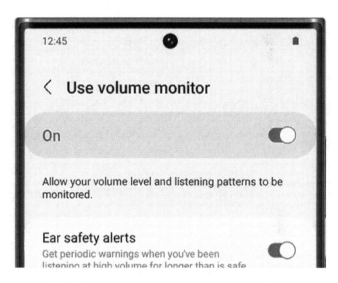

- To get notifications when listening to audio at a high volume for a longer duration, press the switch next to "**Ear safety alerts**."

Use Driving monitor

When you have your Galaxy Ultra paired with your car through Bluetooth, the driving

monitor settings can help you concentrate on
your driving.

- Launch the Settings app.
- Afterward, hit "**Digital Wellbeing and
  parental controls**."
- From there, choose "**Driving
  monitor**."
- If asked, press "**Turn on**," then go
  through the prompts.
- Hit "**Start**."

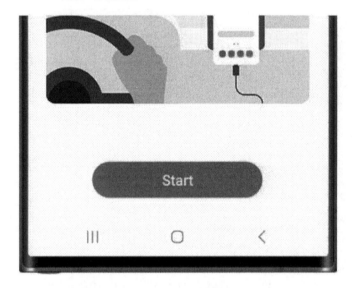

- After that, choose "**Add**" to pick your
  excluded applications.
- Proceed by choosing the applications
  you desire to remove from the Driving
  monitor.
- Afterward, hit "**Done**."
- Once you're set to When you're ready to
  hit the road, choose "**Start**" to

commence using the Driving monitor.
For the duration that your Galaxy Ultra
is paired with your car through
Bluetooth, the Driving monitor will
monitor your phone usage.

Set up Parental controls

Parental control lets guardians manage the
duration their kids spend on their
smartphones, including the applications and
websites they visit.

Create a Samsung account for your child

To control the applications that your kids can
access, you should first create a Samsung
Account for that kid.

- Launch the Settings app.
- Go ahead and select your Samsung account name.
- Then choose "**Family**."
- Afterward, hit "**Add family member**."
- From there, hit "**Create child account**."
- After this, choose "**Next**."
- Review the information that appears, then choose "**Agree**."
- Then choose "**Agree**" once more.

- Proceed by entering your credit card information, then choose "**Verify**."
- However, if you're yet to add a credit card to your account, hit on "**Register card**," then go through the prompts.
- Go ahead and insert your kid's details, then hit "**Create account**."
- Check your kid's email and insert the verification code that was sent there, then hit "**Verify**" to register your kid's account. After that, choose "**Next**."
- When asked about SmartThings Find, hit "**Skip**."
- You'll now be able to choose your kid's account and control the applications they can use. For instance, if you don't want your child to use certain applications, hit "Allowed apps," then press the switch next to the applications. After that, hit "**Block**."

Conclusion

Most of the changes and improvements on the Galaxy S24 Ultra are in the software rather than the physical composition of the device. The improved camera capabilities should be a great addition for lovers of photography, while the latest processor and 12MP RAM will make game lovers and heavy users excited.

I hope you're excited to start maximizing your device. Thanks for reading!!!

About the Author

Shawn Blaine is a gadget reviewer, programmer, and computer geek. He has worked for some big tech companies in the past. He's currently focused on coding and blockchain development but still finds time to write and teach people how to use their smart devices to the fullest.

Index

176